TWELVE STEPS TO PSYCHOLOGICAL GOOD HEALTH

BY

GABRIEL SEGAL

Grosvenor House
Publishing Limited

All rights reserved
Copyright © Gabriel Segal, 2013

The right of Gabriel Segal to be identified as the author of this
work has been asserted by him in accordance with Section 78
of the Copyright, Designs and Patents Act 1988

Cover design Gabriel Segal and Stewart Ferguson [White Dragon]

This book is published by
Grosvenor House Publishing Ltd
28-30 High Street, Guildford, Surrey, GU1 3EL.
www.grosvenorhousepublishing.co.uk

This book is sold subject to the conditions that it shall not, by way of
trade or otherwise, be lent, resold, hired out or otherwise circulated
without the author's or publisher's prior consent in any form of binding or
cover other than that in which it is published and
without a similar condition including this condition being imposed
on the subsequent purchaser.

A CIP record for this book
is available from the British Library

ISBN 978-1-78148-846-1

The Twelve Steps of Alcoholics Anonymous are reprinted and adapted
with permission of Alcoholics Anonymous World Services, Inc. ("AAWS")
Permission to adapt the Twelve Steps does not mean that AAWS has
reviewed or approved the contents of this publication, or that AAWS
necessarily agrees with the views expressed herein. A.A. is a program of
recovery from alcoholism only – use of the Twelve Steps in connection
with program and activities which are patterned after A.A., but which
address other problems, or in any other non-A.A. context, does not imply
otherwise. Additionally, while A.A. is a spiritual program, A.A. is not a
religious program. Thus, A.A. is not affiliated or allied with any sect,
denomination, or specific religious belief.

Some of the quotations, copied from the internet,
have not been verified and may not be strictly accurate.

For Agnes and Mike: spiritual beings

Introduction

This book is a guide to a 12-step programme designed to bring peace of mind, happiness and serenity through the development of psychological good health. It is very closely based on the 12 steps of Alcoholics Anonymous (AA), where they are presented as a way to recover from alcoholism. Close variants of them are used by other 12-step fellowships for recovery from drug and other types of addictions, such as Narcotics Anonymous, Marijuana Anonymous, Cocaine Anonymous, Gambler's Anonymous and Sex and Love Addicts Anonymous. The steps work for alcoholism and drug addiction, and this guide is designed to help alcoholics and addicts through them. But it is meant for anyone who wants to feel better about themselves and the world they live in. For AA's steps are really not about alcohol or addiction, but about how to deal with psychological causes of stress, irritability, discontent and emotional disturbance, through a programme of what we can call 'spiritual' development. The kind of 'spirituality' involved here has nothing essentially to do with any god or anything supernatural, but can be fully understood in naturalistic terms. It is about a psychologically healthy involvement with the world around you and the other sentient, feeling beings that inhabit it.

There is an anonymous quotation: 'Serenity is not freedom from the storm: it is peace within the storm'. The steps show us a way to find that peace. Life brings storms: storms outside you, in the world you inhabit, inside your body, inside your mind. We can't always escape them. But we can always find peace within them, however forceful they are.

The steps are simple. But they are not that easy. You will have to take to heart the basic principles, which are based on the wisdom of Lao Tzu, Buddhism and Stoicism, and be prepared to change the way you think about things and the way you approach life. However, the benefits they bring are enormous. If you do them, you will feel considerably happier, more free of spirit and serene. You will feel better in yourself, and get on better with those around you and really, no one has any valid reason for not doing them, unless they are already content as they are. You have nothing to lose. The steps are free, you can do them in your own time, and they will work for you for the rest of your life.

AA has something of a reputation as being a religious programme. But it need not be seen that way. The way the programme works for alcoholism and drug addiction can be understood entirely in scientific terms.

In the basic text of Alcoholics Anonymous, a book of the same name, usually referred to as "the Big Book," the steps are introduced with these words: "[T]here is One who has all power and that one is God – may you find Him now." Only the first of the twelve steps mentions alcohol and the 12th step includes the words: "Having had a spiritual awakening as the result of these steps..." Thus the Big Book presents the steps as a way to find God and to have something called a 'spiritual awakening'. Recovery from alcoholism is a by-product of the 'spiritual awakening'. In step eleven and throughout the first printing of the first edition of the book, the 'spiritual awakening' is talked of in terms of conscious contact with God. However, in the second printing of the book, in 1941, an appendix on 'Spiritual Experience' was added. Here it says:

> "The terms 'spiritual experience' and 'spiritual awakening' are used many times in this book which, upon careful reading, shows that the personality change sufficient to bring about recovery from alcoholism has manifested itself among us in many different forms.
>
> Yet it is true that our first printing gave many readers the impression that these personality changes, or religious experiences, must be in the nature of sudden and spectacular upheavals. Happily for everyone, this conclusion is erroneous.
>
> In the first few chapters a number of sudden revolutionary changes are described. Though it was not our intention to create such an impression, many alcoholics have nevertheless concluded that in order to recover they must acquire an immediate and overwhelming 'God-consciousness' followed at once by a vast change in feeling and outlook.
>
> Among our rapidly growing membership of thousands of alcoholics such transformations, though frequent, are by no means the rule. Most of

our experiences are what the psychologist William James calls the 'educational variety' because they develop slowly over a period of time. Quite often friends of the newcomer are aware of the difference long before he is himself. He finally realizes that he has undergone a profound alteration in his reaction to life; that such a change could hardly have been brought about by himself alone. What often takes place in a few months could seldom have been accomplished by years of self-discipline. With few exceptions our members find that they have tapped an unsuspected inner resource, which they presently identify with their own conception of a Power greater than themselves.

Most of us think this awareness of a Power greater than ourselves is the essence of spiritual experience. Our more religious members call it 'God-consciousness.'"

The spiritual awakening is described here in terms of a personality change, and a profound alteration in one's reaction to life. It is presented as essentially involving an 'awareness of a Power greater than ourselves' that (only) our 'more religious members' call 'God-consciousness'.

In fact, in the actual steps this 'Power' is referred to as 'God *as we understood Him*', rather than just 'God.' The words '*as we understood Him*' feature thanks to the insistence of founder members Jim Burwell and Hank Pankhurst, who were atheist/agnostic types. I believe that they meant the expression 'God *as we understood Him*' to have an extremely liberal interpretation, along the lines of 'anything you like (other than yourself).'

If we take God out of the equation, we are left with the idea that developing a relationship of some kind to something other than one's self, along the lines presented in the steps, can tap into an unsuspected inner resource, bring about a personality change and a profound alteration in one's reaction to life of a kind that are sufficient even to bring about recovery from alcoholism. I think this is the best way to look at the steps.

The steps (after step one) have nothing to do with alcoholism or addiction per se. Rather they are a way of bringing about a profound alteration in the way one thinks, feels and acts. They do suffice to solve the problems of alcoholism or drug addiction, if one has them. But they are basically a way of achieving and maintaining psychological good health and will be enormously beneficial for anyone struggling with their reactions to life and seeking serenity. This programme will improve anybody's psychological health and peace of mind.

Certainly, the programme deals comprehensively with alcoholism/substance addiction. (Alcoholism is just addiction to alcohol, so whenever I talk of addicts or addiction, I include alcoholics and alcoholism, and when I talk of 'use' of drugs, I include drinking alcohol.) The programme works extremely well for alcoholism. In the Big Book, the main author, Bill Wilson, the genius psychologist and social engineer behind most of the 12-step programme and the magnificent construction of the fellowship of Alcoholics Anonymous itself, wrote: "Rarely have we seen a person fail who has thoroughly followed our path". It is rumoured that he later said that he regretted the 'Rarely' and would rather have said 'never have we seen a person fail who has thoroughly followed our path.' In fact, that story is apocryphal and he never made the stronger claim. But I have done some (informal and unscientific) research that strongly indicates that the programme is in fact 100% effective. I have polled literally many thousands of alcoholics and drug addicts (15–20,000 subjects, mainly on the internet, on *Facebook* and *Google* groups) asking: "Have you done the twelve steps thoroughly and then relapsed while still doing them thoroughly? Or do you know of anyone meeting those conditions?" My sample included not only members of Anonymous fellowships, but also disaffected ex-members who were not satisfied with and indeed are very opposed to the programme and the fellowships. The result was amazingly robust. Only four of the thousands even offered a claim to the effect that they are or knew someone who had done the steps and relapsed while still doing them. Of those four, two quickly changed their minds after a short discussion about exactly how they had been working on each specific step prior to their relapse. One person claimed to know someone who had relapsed while still doing the steps, but was unable to provide any details except to say that her acquaintance has major problems concentrating on any task at all. One other claim remains in place, and that individual admits that he cannot in fact remember what he was doing in the days before he relapsed. The steps work. They really do. Period.

If you are an alcoholic or addict, and you wish to quit, then you should do the steps. There is no reason not to and they will work. They always do. Living without alcohol or drugs may seem to you like an impossibility, or nearly so. You may feel that alcohol or drugs are an essential part of your way of life. You may feel as though alcohol or drugs are your constant companion, or your lover. You may feel that you would not really be yourself without them. You may feel that life would be very drab and dull without them, or very stressful. Do not let such feelings deter you. They are normal for an addict. But they are completely misguided. No matter how intertwined your being and your life are with alcohol or drugs, you can do perfectly well without them. But more than that, you will do much better without them. You will feel ever so much happier that way. There will be no hole, no gap, nothing missing. There will be only more fulfilment, contentment and peace of mind. These are what the steps bring by way of recovery.

If you would like to do some other form of therapy, such as cognitive-behavioural therapy, dialectical-behavioural therapy, emotional freedom technique, psychodynamic therapy, trauma therapy or motivational interviewing, to help, that is fine. But do both that and the steps to maximise your chances of a good and permanent recovery. You do not want to take risks with your life, and relying on anything other than the steps is taking a risk. No other treatment is anywhere close to 100% effective and remember that a therapist will not always be there for you. The fellowships will always be there for you and, given the Internet, they will be available, near enough, at all times and all places. For free, for as long as you live.

The programme is certainly not a magic cure for all psychiatric conditions. But it did completely cure my own previously lifelong problems with depression and anxiety, after years of psychoanalysis and other forms of therapy and prescribed pills had failed completely. Indeed, even the sleeping pills I used did not put me to sleep, and now I sleep just fine without any artificial aids at all. I doubt that the programme will by itself cure all forms of depression or deal with all causes of anxiety, and it will not cure deep personality or mood disorders, for which pills may provide vital help. But it will help anyone who suffers from such problems to deal with them better and feel better than they otherwise would, and to stay free of any flaring up of any condition induced or aggravated by stress. The steps provide one with excellent ways of managing one's life. This applies both to the internal life of the mind, one's emotions and thoughts, and to life in the external world, to one's interactions with people and things.

The steps are not like a mere box of helpful ad hoc techniques, such as one finds in some forms of therapy. Rather, they are based on very profound, though rather simple principles, originating with Lao Tzu, Gautama Buddha and the Stoic philosophers, Marcus Aurelius, Epictetus and Seneca. (As far as I know, Bill Wilson never read any Stoics. But some of the Christian thinkers that influenced him surely would have. He almost certainly encountered Buddhism between 1939, when the Big Book was published, and 1952, the publication date of *The Twelve Steps and Twelve Traditions of Alcoholics Anonymous*. The Buddhist influence on the latter work is very clear and deep.)

Though not a panacea, the programme will significantly improve anyone's psychological health and peace of mind. If you follow the path thoroughly, with application and enthusiasm, you will come to know intuitively how to handle your mind and reactions to the world far better than before. These two aspects are mutually enhancing, in a beneficial circle. The less trouble you get into with people and situations, the less there will be to disturb your mind and the better you manage your mind, the less trouble you will get into with the rest of the world. You will become unafraid of people and of financial insecurity. You will want less and be happier with what you have. You will be content with whom and what you are. You will have greater serenity, freedom and joy.

In this book, I explain in simple terms what the steps are, how they work and what is involved in taking them. Any alcoholic or addict who plans to do the steps should join an appropriate Anonymous fellowship, such as AA or NA, and do the steps guided by a sponsor (this being someone in the fellowship who has already done some, and preferably all, of the steps him- or herself, with a year or more of continuous abstinence and who has a sponsor of their own). If you are atheist or agnostic, don't worry about religious elements of the fellowships. The fellowships are mostly eclectic and different groups and members have different views on the role of theistic beliefs in recovery. The fellowship websites have pamphlets that make all this clear. For example AA's *'A Newcomer Asks'* pamphlet says:

> There's a lot of talk about God, though, isn't there?
>
> The majority of AA members believe that we have found the solution to our drinking problem not

through individual willpower, but through a power greater than ourselves. However, everyone defines this power as he or she wishes. Many people call it God, others think it is the AA group, still others don't believe in it at all. There is room in AA for people of all shades of belief and non-belief.

Some members believe that the steps are primarily a way to find God, and put forward this view to newcomers. If a God quest does not appeal to you, just find groups and a sponsor that suit you and do not refrain from reading the rest of this book! You will find plenty to motivate and interest you and plenty about how to maintain good recovery.

If you are not an alcoholic or addict, or if for some reason you cannot find an appropriate sponsor, you will not need one. But you will need the assistance of someone you trust, such as a doctor, a spiritual leader, an acquaintance or maybe even a carefully selected stranger – someone you trust completely and who will not pass judgement upon you, and someone with whom you do not have much emotional involvement. For a key part of the programme is that you will need to be completely honest about everything both with yourself and with at least one other person. (This element of the programme is based on the Christian confessional, something not prominent in Buddhism or Stoicism, and features in most, if not all, talking therapies). You must face your truth and share it with another.

CHAPTER ONE

Philosophy: Spirituality, Psychology and Science

The Big Book presents alcoholism as a triplex disease, in terms of what it calls a 'physical allergy', a 'mental obsession' and a 'spiritual malady'. I think this articulated 'disease' conception is both very helpful and correct in essence and in detail. The picture contemporary science offers is that the so-called 'physical allergy' appears to be confined to alcoholism and other substance addictions (including addictions to drugs and sugar). The mental obsession appears to be present in all addictions, including behavioural ones and nearly everyone has, to a greater or lesser degree, the 'spiritual malady'. It is an aspect of the human condition. The steps do not cure the 'physical allergy', which is why substance addicts have to remain abstinent. The 'mental obsession', which is very severe in substance addicts, is caused by an interaction of the 'spiritual malady' and the 'physical allergy'. The 'obsession' in behavioural addictions results mainly just from the 'spiritual malady', perhaps interacting with other neurological conditions. The steps deal with the spiritual malady, hence the obsession. This allows addicts to remain abstinent without difficulty and it is because the steps deal with the spiritual malady that they are of value to everyone, and not just addicts. Let us look briefly at each of the three components of the disease.

The 'physical allergy'

The 'physical allergy' simply consists in the phenomenon of drugs or alcohol causing cravings. ('Allergy' is not used here in a medical sense, but just means a strong adverse reaction). When an alcoholic has a drink, this causes a powerful conscious urge, strong desire or felt need for another one. This makes it nigh on impossible for the alcoholic to drink amounts as small as they would want to or intend to when they have their first drink of the day. A true alcoholic pretty much never has just one drink. There is excellent evidence that this phenomenon is based in a neurological condition of the dopamine system, discovered by Terry Robinson and Kent Berridge, called 'incentive sensitization'.

The dopamine system is an evolutionarily primitive, small, but very powerful system in the brain. It is the seat of instinctive drives for food, water and sex. It is the main locus of what is called 'reward learning': when an animal does something that brings more pleasure than expected, this will increase the chances of it repeating the same behaviour, given the same stimulus. When a puppy hears the hint of a sound like that of a can being opened in the kitchen, its ears will prick up, and it will move with tremendous speed and power towards the noise and proceed to indulge in insistent food-seeking behaviour. That is the dopamine system in action. The system becomes attuned to reward cues, and generates motivation to act in a reward-seeking fashion. Berridge and Robinson call this motivational state a 'wanting.' 'Wantings' are probably unconscious, but they often cause or manifest as conscious desires, felt needs or urges.

What happens in true alcoholism and substance addiction is that the dopamine system becomes hypersensitive to cues. The motivation to get a reward becomes abnormally and pathologically powerful: it can manifest as or cause what we ordinarily call 'craving'.

One of the two most powerful triggers for a 'wanting' in alcoholics and addicts is their favoured substance itself. That is why a drink or a drug does not satisfy an addict's craving, desire or felt need, but rather increases it. That is the neurological basis of the 'physical allergy'.

The 'mental obsession'

The 'mental obsession' consists in alcoholics and addicts suffering from very frequent desires, urges or felt needs to drink or use. This phenomenon is also based in the sensitization of the dopamine system. Over time, more and more stimuli become associated with rewarding ingestions, and so more and more situations trigger 'wantings'. Crucially, internal states, feelings, become cues for using. By far the most powerful of these is stress. This is the second major trigger for 'wantings'.

It often happens that an alcoholic or addict manages to achieve a period of sobriety. They have suffered enough from their habit, made a firm decision never to use again, sworn to be abstinent. After a period of weeks or months suddenly an irresistible 'wanting' or desire to use recurs. The 'wanting' wins out, the addict uses; cravings ensue, and then relapse. In typical cases, the 'wanting' wins out not by manifesting as a powerful conscious craving, but rather by inducing a cognitive dysfunction, typically a loss of memory. The alcoholic fancies a drink and either just completely forgets altogether that they are alcoholic and having a drink is seriously risky. Or they will forget the very persuasive reasons they have for believing that a drink is risky, and their minds will construct some absurd rationalization to make them think it is ok to have a drink just this one time. These are cases when the dopamine system beats the cortex, which is the part of the brain responsible for rational thought. Instinctive drive beats higher cognition.

What usually sets off the obsession to end a period of abstinence is (conscious or unconscious) stress caused by unmanaged emotions becoming turbulent. It is important to note that stress is not always accompanied by distress. There is also a phenomenon of happy, or elated stress. (Chemically, both distress stress and happy stress correlate with the release of a stress hormone in the dopamine system itself.) Emotional turbulence is the result of 'spiritual malady'.

The 'spiritual malady'

Symptoms of the spiritual malady, dis-ease, or malaise, are irritability, restlessness, and discontent due to anxiety, fear, resentment, dissatisfaction, low-esteem, guilt, jealousy, loneliness, listlessness, existential angst and the like.

These all stem from overactive, misdirected and unmanaged instincts: excessive instinctive needs, unsatisfied, creating emotional turbulence and disturbance to serenity.

Bill Wilson saw the root of the problem: "Selfishness – self-centredness! That, we think, is the root of our troubles." Selfishness in this context has a very specific meaning. It means, self-seeking, self-absorption and self-will. Self-seeking is placing the satisfaction of one's own desires as the end goal of actions and interactions with others. It is doing things with the ultimate aim of making oneself feel better. A person can be in many ways unselfish and still be self-seeking in this way. They may be thoughtful and generous and considerate. But they treat others well because, at the end of the day, it makes them feel good. They may treat others well, but do not in any meaningful sense treat others as being as important as they are, or place the needs of others ahead of, or even level with, their own. They may act morally, doing what is right. But they do not do what is right just because it is right, but because that is how they feel more comfortable.

Indeed 'people-pleasing' – forever trying to please others, even letting oneself get pushed around – seems superficially to be sacrificing the self for the sake of others. But it really isn't. The goal of this sort of behaviour is typically to make oneself feel a certain way: important, needed or loved and people-pleasing may be used to try to get others to behave in desired ways towards oneself. People-pleasing is actually using others to one's own ends and it is rarely good or healthy for the ones who get pleased.

Self-absorption is focusing attention on and thinking about oneself. It is simply directing one's mind inward, onto itself, rather than outward towards the world and the other sentient beings in it. The self-absorbed individual thinks of other things in terms of how they do or can affect him or herself. They have little interest in how other things are just in themselves.

Self-will is stubborn, excessive adherence to doing things one's own way and trying to have things as one thinks they should be. Self-willed individuals are not inclined to take advice, or listen carefully to the suggestions of others about what they should do. They do not tend to accept moral or other correction. They think they know best what is right. They do their own thing. The self-willed individual tends to put down any inadequate or bad consequences of their actions to something other than themselves. It is always the fault of another person or condition and so they tend not to accept defeat even when it is clear (to everyone else) that they are, in fact defeated.

Most of us are much more selfish than we initially think we are. It takes a good honest look at the way we look at things, the way we see our place among others, and at the true motives for our actions, before we can see the true nature and extent of our selfishness. There is no shame in being selfish. It is not our fault if we are – especially if we have not even noticed that we are. If we face up to our selfishness, rather than pretending it does not exist, we can do something about it, and benefit enormously from the result.

Here is a little example of a technique you can use if some tragedy has struck, in the recent or distant past and you are caught up in emotional pain as a result. Instead of dwelling on just how much you hurt right now, reflect upon just how much terrible suffering there is in the world. People have just learnt they have cancer, or the love of their life has just left them for another, or died, or their parents have been murdered, or their only child has died, or their children insist that they hate them, take drugs and disappear, or their child has been raped, or they themselves have just been raped – and so on and on and on. Nearly every adult has lost a loved one. What you call your suffering, that you are so focussed on, that is taking up so much of your awareness, is just a tiny, tiny fragment of all this. You don't even have to think of it as yours, particularly, if you don't wish to. It is just a miniscule speck of that great suffering that there is in the world. You just happen be aware of it at the moment. You don't have to let it take you over. So don't. Unwrap yourself from it. Distance yourself from it. Turn your attention away from it and toward something else: look out at the world. Take a leaf from the diary of Anne Frank, a Jewish girl, in her early teens, living in The Netherlands under Nazi occupation, who advised: "Think of all the beauty still left around you and be happy."

This little thought process makes it easier to live with one's emotional distress. It requires a move away from an egocentric picture of the situation, which consists just in oneself and one's pain, and a move towards a quite different, other-focussed picture in which the pain is just a small element of the world's suffering, and the person is just one consciousness among millions, within whose view that tiny pain happens to appear.

It is not hard to see how self-seeking and self-will relate to alcoholism and other drug use. The selfish individual is preoccupied with their own feelings and forever engaged in trying to adjust the world so it makes them feel better. As a life strategy, this simply does not work because reality is very hard to shift. Other people rarely feel and behave just as one wants and good things (other than water) do not rain from the sky. As the strategy fails, the selfish individual turns to drugs or alcohol as a quick, easy and direct fix for their feelings. With such substances, the individual can become God of their own feelings and so rule the realm that matters to them most. They can do things their own way to have things their own way. And if they learn to do this early in life, as the vast majority of serious addicts do (in the emotional turbulence of early teens), they never learn to deal with their feelings properly. They are used to getting high or anaesthetised and substance use becomes their only coping strategy. If they have vulnerable dopamine systems, these will become sensitized and they will become true addicts in the strongest sense of the term.

Addicts are not necessarily more selfish than other people. They start out using drugs to alter their feelings and, for whatever reason, their dopamine system, which is the seat of instinctive drives, becomes damaged and oversensitive to drug-cues. When sensitized and deprived of drug-induced stimulation, it induces a state of 'faux starvation' in the poor sufferer, and makes him or her feel she really needs the drug.

The phenomenon of true addiction – rooted in a malfunctioning dopamine system – just brings into sharp relief a kind of maladjustment that is extremely widespread. Self-seeking and self-will combine to give rise to behavioural 'addictions' to romance, gambling, work, exercise and all manner of other things, from obsessively looking at property prices to watching soap operas on TV or collecting stamps or friends on Facebook. All of these are used to escape from disturbing feelings, and most involve a desperate and misplaced attempt to satisfy some instinctive need: money for food and material possessions, or love or power or the esteem of others.

These activities do not succeed in their aim of satisfying the selfish individual's instinctive felt needs or desires. This is because, wrapped up in their own feelings, they are unable to engage and interact in an emotionally satisfying way with the people and things with which their behaviours are involved. The self-willed individual then just keeps on trying and failing with the same strategies and 'addictive' behaviour results.

The spiritual malady leads to problems in all the important areas of life. It leads to relationship problems as the individual tries to cause the partner to feel and act in ways that will make them feel good, instead of treating the other and his or her feelings as ends-in-themselves, as being as important or more important than the subject and their own feelings. This applies to all relationships: romantic, familial and friendship. By focusing on their own feelings, the selfish person is hampered in their ability to listen to others properly and learn from them.

Their sensitivity to and awareness of the feelings of others is impaired and so they cannot be truly close to them. When it comes to romance, they will end up in unsatisfying or bad relationships or alone.

The same will apply to their work. The selfish person does not put effort into work because the product benefits others, nor, more abstractly, because it makes the world a better place. This undermines incentive to do as good a job as one can and it detracts from the satisfaction that doing a job well brings to less selfish individuals. If a selfish person works hard it is in the pursuit of material wealth, other-esteem or power, or just escape from inner distress. In such a case, hard work does not bring satisfaction or serenity.

The same applies to an individual's relationship with their physical environment. The selfish person tends to look at the environment in terms of its affordances for pleasure, asking themselves: 'what can it do for me?' This general approach detracts from the individual's capacity to appreciate it for what it is. A selfish person in a lovely forest, for example, will tend (maybe subconsciously) to think along the lines of: can I eat it, take a bit and sell it, bring a boyfriend here to make him amenable to romance, use it for shelter in an emergency or use it in some other way? They may wish to own some or all of it, so it becomes theirs to do with as they will. If the forest provides no such affordances, then a selfish person will fail to see a point to it. They will attend to the feelings within them, and not to the beauty of the ponds and trees around them. A selfless person is able to interact with the forest cognitively and emotionally in a quite different way: they can simply appreciate its beauty and take joy in being there with it. Accepting that one is just a tiny part of a great universe, a single consciousness with a capacity to experience the ambient environment, brings far more pleasure and satisfaction than wanting or trying to play God with it.

Spirituality, as I use the term, is simply the opposite of self-absorption, self-seeking and self-will. The spiritually fit person treats their feelings as modes of contact with other people and elements of the world around them and as guides to proper interactions with them. The spiritually fit person humbly accepts others and the rest of the world as they are, and goes with the flow. The spiritually fit person tries to change their mind to fit the word, and not the other way around. That is the central principle of the philosophies of Lao Tzu, Buddha and the Stoics. Lau Tzu puts it thus: "He who knows that enough is enough will always have enough," and, "[b]e content with what you have; rejoice in the way things are. When you realize there is nothing lacking, the whole world belongs to you." And Buddha: "Peace comes from within. Do not seek it without."

Spirituality opens your mind to the world as it is, brings connectedness to it and allows you to live properly and contentedly as a mere tiny inhabitant of it.

AA itself is an amazing fellowship that was born in 1935 and has flourished and grown since then. The current membership is about 2,000,000. Part of the reason for its excellent health as an organization is that members put the group first. It is held together by twelve traditions, and the first of these says: "Each member of Alcoholics Anonymous is but a small part of a great whole. A.A. must continue to live or most of us will surely die. Hence our common welfare comes first. But individual welfare follows close afterward". The second tradition includes the words: "Our leaders are but trusted servants".

In many important ways, humans have evolved to live in groups far more than have most other animals. This applies to all social situations: we are each just one member of a family, a business, a nation and so on. Groups work best where leaders are but trusted servants. We each have our roles to play as just one member of each of our groups. One of the unique characteristics of our species is that individuals have very specialised roles and abilities: one person knows how to grow tomatoes, another knows how to build planes, a third to fly them. As individuals, we flourish when we aim to play our roles in our groups, let others play theirs, and do not try to exploit them to our own ends. This is not to say that we should identify ourselves with or define ourselves by our specialised roles, nor that we should aim to pick just one or two to give our lives purpose. We should not. It is just to say that we do best in groups, and best when we put the group first and ourselves second.

Spiritual malady is endemic in our species. We tend to be dominated by self-seeking and self-will. As a result, in a world in which we could all flourish, we are surrounded by war, crime, drugs and starvation and we are destroying the very environment that nurtures us (asking what it can do for us, not what we can do for it). We owe it to ourselves to get better.

The world would be a better place for all of us if we heeded the words of Albert Einstein: "A human being is a part of a whole, called by us 'universe', a part limited in time and space. He experiences himself, his thoughts and feelings as something separated from the rest... a kind of optical delusion of his consciousness. This delusion is a kind of prison for us, restricting us to our personal desires and to affection for a few persons nearest to us. Our task must be to free ourselves from this prison by widening our circle of compassion to embrace all living creatures and the whole of nature in its beauty." And why procrastinate? "How wonderful it is that nobody need wait a single moment before starting to improve the world," –Anne Frank.

I think there are many reasons why we are so much more prone to spiritual sickness than other animals. The most significant one perhaps, is that we develop so slowly. As babies, we can do almost nothing for ourselves. We are full of needs and surrounded by giants who do not always fulfil them at our command. We are powerless and vulnerable. Being a human infant is a traumatic experience for all of us. No wonder we are so messed up!

Chapter Two

The Steps Introduced

To anticipate what follows, here are some variants or formulations of the steps that you can use and refer back to as you work through the book. We can think of the different sets as different verbal formulations of the very same steps, just different words used to express the same basic ideas and principles. Or, if by 'steps' we refer to the actual words and sentences, as written, then the different sets are sets of different steps. But they are variants of one another, and all are variants of the ones AA originally formulated. So, for example AA step one reads: "We admitted we were powerless over alcohol – that our lives had become unmanageable". NA step one reads: "We admitted we were powerless over our addiction, that our lives had become unmanageable". We could call these different formulations of the very same step, since the action required is the same whether one is addicted to alcohol or to something else. Or, if by 'step' we refer to the actual wording, we could say they are variant steps. It makes no significant difference which convention one adopts.

The original formulation of Alcoholics Anonymous:

1. We admitted we were powerless over alcohol – that our lives had become unmanageable.
2. Came to believe that a Power greater than ourselves could restore us to sanity.
3. Made a decision to turn our will and our lives over to the care of God *as we understood Him*.
4. Made a searching and fearless moral inventory of ourselves.
5. Admitted to God, to ourselves and to another human being the exact nature of our wrongs.
6. Were entirely ready to have God remove all these defects of character.
7. Humbly asked Him to remove our shortcomings.
8. Made a list of all persons we had harmed, and became willing to make amends to them all.
9. Made direct amends to such people wherever possible, except when to do so would injure them or others.
10. Continued to take personal inventory and when we were wrong promptly admitted it.
11. Sought through prayer and meditation to improve our conscious contact with God *as we understood Him*, praying only for knowledge of His will for us and the power to carry that out.
12. Having had a spiritual awakening as the result of these steps, we tried to carry this message to alcoholics and to practice these principles in all our affairs.

General schematic formulation:

1. We admitted we were powerless over X – that our lives had become unmanageable.
2. Came to believe that a power greater than ourselves could restore us to sanity.
3. Made a decision to turn our will and our lives over to a higher power.
4. Made a searching and fearless moral inventory of ourselves.
5. Admitted to a higher power (if appropriate), to ourselves and to another human being the exact nature of our wrongs.
6. Were entirely ready to live without all these defects of character.
7. Adopted a practice of humility, so that our shortcomings might be overcome.
8. Made a list of all persons we had harmed, and became willing to make amends to them all.
9. Made direct amends to such people wherever possible, except when to do so would injure them or others.
10. Continued to take personal inventory and when we were wrong promptly admitted it.
11. Sought through prayer and/or meditation and reflection to improve our conscious contact with a higher power, seeking only for knowledge of right action and the power to carry that out.
12. Having had a spiritual awakening as the result of these steps, we tried to carry this message to others and to practice these principles in all our affairs.

Formulation for non-addicts:

1. We admitted that we could not manage our behaviour, minds or lives.
2. Came to believe that a power greater than ourselves could restore us to rationality and mental balance.
3. Made a decision to turn our will and our lives over to the care of a power greater than ourselves.
4. Made a searching and fearless moral inventory of ourselves.
5. Admitted to ourselves and to another human being the exact nature of our wrongs.
6. Were entirely ready to live without all these defects of character.
7. Humbly became prepared so to do.
8. Made a list of all persons we had harmed, and became willing to make amends to them all.
9. Made direct amends to such people wherever possible, except when to do so would injure them or others.
10. Continued to take personal inventory, and when we were wrong, promptly admitted it.
11. Adopted practices of prayer and/or reflection and meditation to deepen our understanding of our place in the universe and how we might best conduct ourselves as parts of it.
12. Having had a spiritual awakening as the result of these steps, we tried to carry this message to others who sought spiritual health, and to practice these principles in all our affairs.

Author's preferred formulation:

1. We admitted we were powerless over our affliction – that our lives had become unmanageable.
2. Came to believe that a power greater than ourselves could restore us to sanity.
3. Made a decision to turn our will and our lives over to the universe and go with its flow.
4. Made a searching and fearless moral inventory of ourselves.
5. Admitted to ourselves and to another human being the exact nature of our wrongs.
6. Were entirely ready to give up all these defects of character.
7. Adopted a practice of humility so that our shortcomings might be overcome.
8. Made a list of all persons we had harmed, and became willing to make amends to them all.
9. Made direct amends to such people wherever possible, except when to do so would injure them or others.
10. Continued to take personal inventory and when we were wrong promptly admitted it.
11. Sought through reflection and meditation to improve our conscious contact with the universe and its inhabitants, seeking for knowledge of how to act rightly and strength to do so.
12. Having had a spiritual awakening as the result of these steps, we tried to carry this message to others afflicted, and to practice these principles in all our affairs.

TWELVE STEPS TO PSYCHOLOGICAL GOOD HEALTH

Don't concern yourself much about the differences between the sets of steps at this point. They will make more sense as you work through the programme. Just pick the one that suits you best for now, and adjust later if you feel like. You can fill in the blanks and tweak the generic version, to suit yourself, if you fancy doing that.

The basic outline of the programme is as follows. First, on step one, you will admit that you cannot win your battle, whether it be against the bottle, the addiction, the emotional dysfunction or destructive thoughts or behaviour patterns that are troubling you. You have tried battling it and consistently lost. Right now is the time to admit defeat. If you are not an addict or do not feel particularly powerless over anything, but you do feel that you are not fully at ease with yourself and the world, and you would like to come to relate to yourself and the world in new way, with more acceptance and joy, and you wish to experience lightness of heart and serenity, then you can skip step one and go straight on to step two.

On step two, you will accept that new interaction with someone or something other than yourself can get you back to sanity, or good mental balance. On step three, you will make a decision to stop running on self-will and turn your will and life over to the care of something else, which we will call a 'higher power': a God of your understanding, or a fellowship, other people in general, some specific other people, the universe – an ideal such as truth, the goodness of humanity, love, good orderly direction, the twelve steps, the Tao or the Dharma way – or a symbolic object or person of your choice (e.g. a the sun, the sea, a dead ancestor, a tree or John Lennon).

It doesn't matter what you choose, you can change your higher power later. The key thing at this point is to commit seriously to doing the rest of the steps properly and thoroughly, no matter what it takes. Initiating and then developing a relationship with a power outside yourself will help you tap into the inner resources you need to follow the programme successfully, recover from your affliction and find serenity.

It is at step four that the real work of recovery, of spiritual health and fitness training, begins. On step four, you will, to the best of your ability, make a list of all instances where your character defects (or shortcomings) have, through instinctive overdrive, caused you emotional disturbance. These will be instances where such things as resentment, fear, envy, greed or pride have caused trouble. You will process these, for example, by learning to forgive yourself and others, put the past behind you and move on. On step five, you will share all this with someone else. On steps six and seven, you will pause to reorient your approach to yourself and your place in the world and reset your goals in life. On steps eight and nine, you will do all you can to fix any harms you have done. Then you will be done with your first pass through the steps. The remaining steps – ten, eleven and twelve – are about maintaining good spiritual or psychological health and continuing the process of spiritual, psychological or character development.

The disease of substance addiction is analogous to permanent physical injury, such as a torn cruciate ligament. If you build up the muscles supporting the knee joint, you can function normally, run and dance. But you have to do physiotherapy every day to keep the muscles strong. If you don't, then your knee will give out and you will fall over. If you are a substance addict you have a damaged dopamine system. You can make up for this by keeping your emotional and relevant higher cognitive functions in good shape. But you have to keep up the mental exercise regime: steps ten, eleven and twelve. If you don't then, under pressure, the dopamine system will kick off, tell you that you want to use, and your memory and/or thought processes will become impaired, you will use and this will almost certainly precipitate a further breakdown with cravings. You will use, wake up feeling terrible, desperate for more, and you will have no resources to resist.

A different analogy, also useful, likens doing the steps to driving. When you first do them, you learn to drive safely along the roads of life. You learn to adjust your thoughts and actions so that you can safely negotiate all the different conditions, including hazardous ones: disappointments, losses, causes of over-excitement and so on. If conditions get easy and you switch on cruise control and don't pay attention to what you are doing, don't keep your eyes and mind on the road, then when a hazard suddenly looms, you will crash. If your spouse walks out on you, you win a bonanza on a lottery or something else springs a turbulent emotion on you, you will forget yourself and pick up. If you get into a habit of cruising along in a dozy state, then even a small bump and will cause you to lose control.

The steps are simple, but they are not easy. It is not easy to face up to the worst parts of yourself. But it is really worth it. You will feel much, much better for it. If you are afraid of doing this, that is very understandable. But then there is all the more reason to do it. You will not benefit from hiding yourself from yourself and living in conscious or unconscious fear of what is inside your own mind. Nor should you run away from guilt and shame, fury, schadenfreude, fear, envy or feelings of inadequacy. It is repressing these unpleasant things and not facing up to them and dealing with them that is the root of much of your discontent. By doing the steps, you will clear your mind of these sources of discontent and come to learn intuitively to catch them as they re-emerge and nip them in the bud. You will come to accept yourself as you are and to like or even love yourself. That is the way to find serenity and joy, and if you are an alcoholic or addict, you will lose any desire to drink or use. Emotional turbulence will not trigger your dopamine system. You will be serene and happy as you are, and so not feel any need to change the way you feel. You will be free!

The steps are in the order they are in for good reason. Each step is but one step. Progress is just one step at a time. As you start out, it is best not to think about the whole programme, about all you are going to have to do, if you are going to do it all. For example, don't worry now about step nine, making amends. The time to think about that is later. For now, just put it out of your mind. When the time comes, things will seem different to you. As with any task, the best course is to focus on the job at hand, and not worry about what you will be doing in the future. The future is the future. Now is now. Now just have a look at step one and think only about that.

Chapter Three

Step By Step

Step One: *powerlessness, unmanageability.*

"By letting it all go it all gets done. The world is won by those who let it go. But when you try and try... the world is beyond winning."
– Lao Tzu

I can't help you much with taking this step, either you are well and truly beaten and it is time for you finally to see what is staring you in the face, or you are not. If you are a substance addict, how many times have you set out with the intention of having just so much and ended up having just so very much more? How many times were you going to quit or cut down tomorrow, or next week, or definitely soon, only to end up using more than ever? WAKE UP! The time to change is NOW.

If you are not a substance addict, for how long have you battled your problems with behaviour, thoughts or emotions in vain, or just waited for things to go differently, only to find that it never changes? How much time have you spent obsessively doing your thing over and over, only to find that however much satisfaction you might get for a few moments, that felt need, that compulsion, just comes right back and sets you off on the chase again? How many times did you decide to do things differently tomorrow or just waited for yourself to change? This has not happened has it? Face reality! Things won't change by themselves. You need to do something differently now. Your behaviour is controlling you, you are not controlling it. It is staring you in the face. Open your eyes. WAKE UP! The time to change is NOW.

How many times have you made the same mistakes with your romantic partner – your boyfriends, girlfriends, lovers or spouse? How many times have you messed up your relationships with friends, or work colleagues? How many times have you found yourself in a fight or altercation or dispute or sulk? How many times has all that anger flared up, taking you over and doing your thinking for you? How many times have you desperately acted to please another, sacrificing yourself, conceding what you should not, giving too much, letting yourself be trampled on, to avoid rejection or retaliation, rather than because it is the right action to take? Your behaviour is controlling you, you are not controlling it. It is staring you in the face. Open your eyes. WAKE UP! The time to submit is NOW.

How much time have you wasted being irritable, restless and discontent? Are you still, now, after all these years, unable to get a good night's sleep? Are you forever listless? Are you forever dwelling on the past, devastated by the loss of your one true love, or parent, or brother? How much time have you wasted being furious at someone else for what they have done to you? How much time have you wasted worrying about what might be, instead of just enjoying being? Your misery has taken you over. It is in control of your mind. It is staring you in the face. Open your eyes. WAKE UP! The time to change is NOW.

Things are not ok with you. They haven't been, not for long time. Maybe they have never been. You are not happy. You have been trying to fill your inner void, or cope with your fear, or your feeling of deprivation, or get rid of your anger or turbulence, or of your feeling of just not being good enough or mattering enough. You have been trying to deal with your problem the wrong way. It has not worked. It has gone very badly wrong. Your way isn't working. It has taken you over. You have become a slave. You have lost the battle. Give it up! Admit defeat. It is time to try something else.

"To do the same thing over and over again is not only boredom: it is to be controlled by rather than to control what you do."
– Heraclitus

Homework

1. Write between 500 and 1,000 words on why you feel powerless over your substance, addiction or mental affliction.
2. Write between 500 and 1,000 words on the way your thoughts, emotions and behaviour have become unmanageable.
3. For alcoholics/addicts: write a sentence or two about how one drink or drug leads to more, and about what happened on occasions when you tried to go without your substance for a while.

Step Two: *belief, insanity*

"I doubt if a single individual could be found from the whole of mankind free from some form of insanity. The only difference is one of degree. A man who sees a gourd and takes it for his wife is called insane because this happens to very few people."
– Desiderius Erasmus

If you are an addict and have taken step one, the idea that you have been insane should not present a problem for you. Think about how many times you made the same mistakes, over and over again. Think about how insanely you overvalued drink and/or drugs. It seemed to you to be the most important thing in the whole world. Perhaps you thought it was the very best thing in the world, your only true companion, your only true love. You felt you really needed it. You just had to have it. Then and only then would things be ok.

Well the great news is: that is crazy thinking. It is just not true. Millions of people have been where you are and got better. You are no different. You are not alone. If you accept help, then you will soon be able to live happily without your constant companion. Indeed you will be far happier without it. You have everything to gain and precisely nothing whatever to lose.

If you are not an addict, then just pause to reflect on how often you have made the same old mistakes and how screwed up your thinking has been. You are not alone. If you accept guidance, then your thinking will straighten out. You will feel no need or compulsion to cling to old patterns of thought and behaviour. You will come to act more constructively and feel better as a result.

"What we actually learn, from any given set of circumstances, determines whether we become increasingly powerless or more powerful."
– Blaine Lee

Homework

1. Write between 200 and 400 words on the way or ways in which your thinking and behaviour in relation to your problem has been insane.
2. Take a moment to reflect on the fact that recovery really is possible, and, that if you accept help, then you too can recover. In your own words, put the thought into writing.

Step Three: *higher power*

"Life is a series of natural and spontaneous changes. Don't resist them; that only creates sorrow. Let reality be reality. Let things flow naturally forward in whatever way they like."
– Lao Tzu

Addictive behaviour is by its nature very self-willed. Many addicts take illegal drugs, putting their own way of doing things ahead of the law. Most societies regard being constantly drunk or out-of-it on drugs as a very bad way of being. But addicts stubbornly insist on doing things their own way: they insist that they know what is right, at least for themselves, and damn it to anyone who thinks differently. The Big Book says 'any life run on self-will can hardly be a success'. This is a sage remark of which everyone, especially addicts, should to take notice.

When self-will combines with self-seeking, an excessive desire to make oneself feel better, as if that mattered more than anything else and this leads to a habit of years of 'self-medication' of one's feelings with drink or drugs, the result is total catastrophe. The addict tries to be God of the only realm that really matters, his own inner world, and fails disastrously. The kingdom of self has truly become the bondage of self. Willingness, honesty and open-mindedness are all you need to allow your self to go free of its own bondage.

In very early recovery, when an addict has only just stopped using, their minds are still functioning poorly due both to the effects of drink or drugs and to the disease itself. It is time to stop wilfully and fearfully clinging to old ways of functioning and it is time to stop trying to rely only on yourself. Join a fellowship, get a sponsor and take advice from those who know how to get and stay clean and sober. It is also a very good idea to select a few people to act as a sort of unofficial advisory board. If you can, pick on people who you think of as wise, or sensible, perhaps ones who know you well, and get into the habit of consulting with them about all important decisions. The unofficial advisory board should include your sponsor, if you have one. But a good sponsor is only a guide through the steps and should not try to take over much of your life. So it is best to have others from whom you can seek advice as well.

As far as possible, take their advice. This will make your life easier and take a load off of your mind. It is also an excellent exercise in letting go of self-will and going with the flow.

When you first join a fellowship, go to a lot of meetings: preferably at least 90 meetings in 90 days. If you don't initially like them, just keep going. At first, it may be hard to find much in common with the other people in the meeting. You may feel they are just not like you. They may seem like aliens to you. Deep down, you may feel like a child surrounded by adults, a child who can't grow up or really just does not want to. You may find it hard to listen to what the others are saying and hard to have much emotional contact with them. This is partly because in very early recovery people tend to be deeply self-absorbed, bound up with their own concerns, locked in their own minds and not at all open to or receptive to the thoughts and feelings of others. The people there are like you and you are like them, in the ways that really matter. But sometimes it takes time for a newcomer to feel that way. Keep going, focus on points of identification with others there and ignore differences between you and them. Bear in mind that the people there are real people with real feelings of their own, all with their own lives and personalities. Try to listen to their shares and take an interest in them as people. Do not try to evaluate or judge what they say. Just listen and find points of identification where you can. You will start relating to the others, to enjoy and benefit from hearing from them. Be patient, give them a chance. Give yourself a chance.

Anybody should be able to recognize some power greater or 'higher' than him or herself. Religious people should have no difficulty facing up to the idea that they are not in a position to argue with God and it is no good pretending otherwise. There are other things that any human, but specially the more self-willed among us, should recognize as guides to action that cannot rationally be argued with: good orderly direction, truth, reality, the universe itself. One cannot do better than have the intellectual humility to follow the dictates of such guides. After all, you are not God and you do not run the universe.

It is a lot harder to swim upstream than to float downstream. You will be stronger if you understand your place in the universe, show some humility and let

yourself be guided by something greater than yourself. To get free of the bondage of your self, you need to turn your will and your life over to the care of some power greater than your self. Let go and go with the flow. "Be like water".
– Bruce Lee

For now, you only need to make a decision to do this and to take the next step in the right direction. Pick a higher power from the above list, or, if you prefer, something else that appeals to you: for example, a group, a fellowship, the human species, human goodness, love, the Dharma way, the Tao, your unofficial advisory board, a dead ancestor, a hero, the twelve steps, the sun or the sea. Whatever you like: the choice is yours.

Make a decision to take the rest of the twelve steps as thoroughly as you can. You are worth it!

"Supreme excellence consists in breaking the enemy's resistance without fighting."
– Sun Tzu

If you are religious, it is time for a prayer. Using the word 'God' to represent your own higher power, one or both of the following would be apt.

"God, I offer myself to thee – to build with me and do with me as Thou wilt. Relieve me of the bondage of self, that I may better do Thy will. Take away my difficulties, that victory over them may bear witness to those I would help of Thy Power, Thy Love and Thy Way of life. May I do Thy will always!"

"God, grant me the serenity to accept the things I cannot change; courage to change the things I can, and wisdom to know the difference. Thy will, not mine, be done."

If you are not religious, you might do well to say one of the prayers anyway, as an act of humility and an expression of hope. But if you don't want to, then don't. Say instead:

"May I have the serenity to accept the things I cannot change; courage to change the things I can, and wisdom to know the difference. May I be free of the bondage of self"

No more procrastination, you have wasted enough of your life doing that! It is time to start getting better. Right now. Remember these words of Marcus Aurelius: "The first rule is to keep an untroubled spirit. The second is to look things in the face and know them for what they are." Now, take action: proceed to step four.

Step four: *inventory*

"You have power over your mind – not outside events. Realize this, and you will find strength."
– Marcus Aurelius

The terms 'defects', 'wrongs' and 'shortcomings' are used synonymously in the original AA formulation of the steps. They simply refer to aspects of our character, maladjustments, that we would be better off without. None of us is perfect. So, in the terminology we are using, we are all defective. It is convenient to think of our main defects as pride, greed, anger, lust, envy, gluttony and sloth. All of these traits are manifestations of excessive concern for the self and they all stem from overactive instincts: to be leader of the pack, to get food and shelter, to breed the most successful offspring, to defend, to rest. But, when overactive, misdirected and unmanaged the instincts lead us to think, feel and act in ways that disturb our serenity. They lead in obvious ways to fear, disappointment, dissatisfaction, guilt, self-pity and mental and, sometimes, physical pain.

Overactive and misdirected instincts often lead to addictive-like behaviour in relation to all kinds of things other than drugs. Food and sex are obvious examples (gluttony and lust). We tend to use anger, self-pity, the esteem of others, money or possessions like drugs, getting kicks or getting momentary escape from something within us that is the real cause of our distress. But because these things do not address the underlying problems, or the inner void, the technique does not work, no amount is enough and we just do the same thing again and again and want more and more.

The solution is to become content with who and what we are. Food and water, shelter and good relations with others are all we need for true happiness. The less defective we are, the less we suffer. The more we live without our defects, the more serene, joyous and free we become.

Letting our defects go is not easy. But it is possible and we are very fortunate indeed that there is a way we can do this. The first and crucial step is to take an inventory. This is simply a fact-finding mission. The aim is not to blame oneself, or others, or anything. It is not to pass judgement on oneself or others. Quite the reverse. The aim is simply to discover the facts, accept, and then forgive everyone for everything. Imperfection in ourselves and others is simply the way of things and there is absolutely no need at all to make ourselves suffer because of it. Causing or even just accepting needless suffering is a mug's game.

The Inventory

In the inventory we look over our history insofar as it is now affecting us adversely. We list specific events, people or things with which we are or have been physically or emotionally involved. We see how we are letting events, people and things that are outside of us disturb our serenity and we look into ourselves to see how excesses of our instincts have been involved in causing the disturbance, as part of the process of easing that disturbance.

The inventory consists in five columns. The first column lists the person, event or thing involved. The second, how this person, event or thing caused the disturbance. The third column describes the aspect of one's self that is affected. The fourth column lists what part, if any; we ourselves played in causing the trouble. The fifth column lists or elaborates on how our defects are involved.

1. Who or what.
2. The cause.
3. Aspect of character affected.
4. My mistakes.
5. Defects involved.

We begin with resentments. Bill W. says that resentment is: "the number one offender. It destroys more alcoholics than anything else". Buddha's view is: "Holding on to anger is like grasping a hot coal with the intent of throwing it at someone else; you are the one who gets burned" and "[t]hose who are free of resentful thoughts surely find peace." And Epictetus tells us how to free ourselves of those resentful thoughts: "When you are offended at any man's fault, turn to yourself and study your own failings. Then you will forget your anger."

Here is a made-up example, involving a fictional character, Joe, and his brother Fred.

1. My brother, Fred.
2. Fred got drunk and kept interrupting me and talking over me at dinner with our parents.
3. Self-esteem.

4. I was trying to show off, making clear to everyone just how successful I have recently been at work.
5. Self-important, self-seeking, insensitive.

In this case, Joe had gone to dinner, happy that he had been promoted because of a good performance at work over the past year. He had been particularly keen to share his joy with the family. In the event, this did not go too well because whenever he got going on the topic, his drunken brother had started blethering on about something else. How thoughtless and insensitive! How unfair! What an asshole! This had been infuriating, and the anger lingered on. In writing the inventory, Joe came to see that the motive of sharing his joy at his success was all mixed up with the motive of getting satisfaction from the esteem of his parents and brother. Thus he had been self-important and self-seeking and he had attempted to present himself as better than his brother, in front of their own parents.

The point of the exercise was for Joe to heal himself and get rid of the disturbance to his own serenity, caused by Fred's behaviour. He reflected that Fred's bad behaviour would probably have been caused by some disturbance in Fred's own mind, some unhappiness or distress. But, whatever, Fred's motives, were entirely beside the point. It was not up to Joe to play the psychoanalyst. So he resisted any temptation to speculate about what might have been going on in Fred's mind.

Rather, he made an effort to adopt a sympathetic view of Fred as a fellow human being and a brother, to forgive him in his own mind, and to wish the best for him. Had he been religious, he would certainly have said a prayer for him.

Joe realised that he had been trying to manipulate the thoughts and behaviour of others to the end of making himself seem better, to bolster his own self-esteem. The result had been that he had ended up frustrated and resentful. He then went on to forgive himself: "I am only human, I make mistakes. Never mind. It is all done now. The past can't be changed, so there is precisely no point wasting time and emotional well-being by regretting it. Put it behind me, move on, and make sure to try to avoid making the same mistake again."

"Do not let the behaviour of others destroy your inner peace."
– Dalai Lama

Key points to bear in mind when doing the resentment inventory are as follows:

1. This is absolutely not an exercise in trying to get clear about what really happened. The actual facts of the original events are probably not knowable and even if they are, they will appear differently in different people's perspectives on them. Even if the factual details could be established, they would likely appear very different from Fred's perspective than from Joe's, their parents or that of a neutral party. The actual facts of the case are completely irrelevant. The problem is your perception of

the event and the stress that it is causing you, and these are what need do to be dealt with.
2. The motives of other people are equally irrelevant. If other people have done wrong it is because of their own issues and has nothing to do with you. If they wanted to hurt you, either you did something to set this off or you did not. In either case, the hurt is the result of pathology: either just in the other person or in both of you.
3 Therefore, blame has no place in your mind or in the universe. Do not blame the other or yourself. Blame is just the manifestation of mental pathology. It has no value at all and is entirely destructive. Forget it. Forgive the other, forgive yourself. You are not a judge. You are a clinician, and your patient is yourself.
4. The past cannot be changed. But it is completely gone and cannot affect you adversely, unless you, yourself, allow it to do so. So be smart, let it go and move on!
5. Move on in a positive way, with the aim of making things better for others and for yourself.

You should aim to do an inventory for every case in which a defect, an overactive instinct, has, directly or indirectly through your actions, been involved in causing disturbance to your serenity. Do one for your fears. If you have just recently become abstinent from drink or drugs, then you will have to start dealing with fear. Allow yourself to feel it. It really isn't that bad. Do not fear fear. Fear is like anger, useful only for flight or defence, in moments of immediate danger. Do not let it linger. Start dealing properly with situations that cause it, instead of running away or pretending they do not exist. Fear often interacts with sloth to cause all kinds of problems. Take a deep breath and make that appointment with the dentist. Open those bills. Start working on the project that you have been avoiding for fear of failure or of success. Use the inventory to get clear and realistic about your fears, and to help you let them go.

Do an inventory working through the harms you have done to others, to make sure that conscious and unconscious guilt is expunged as far as possible and do one for envy. Suppose for example you are envious of someone because they have just bought a very expensive beautiful house. Why does it bother you that someone else has something nice? Is it affecting your self-esteem? Is it bringing up some fear you have? Does it make you feel disappointed in yourself? Remember that their having the great house does not make you have any less, or be any less. Be happy for them. Take pleasure in the beauty of the house itself. Be glad that it exists and that someone is living in it. That the nice house exists and that he lives in it make the world a better place. It is the world you, yourself, inhabit too, so be glad for it.

Be thorough and fearless. Make sure to include everything that you think might possibly be a cause of turbulence, however small. No niggle is too trivial to include. If in doubt, inventory it. But once you have written down everything you can think of, move on. Don't obsess over making sure your inventory is complete before proceeding to the remainder of the steps. You need to be getting on with things. You can always come back to the inventory later, if you remember something that should be included.

The world is also a better place for having you in it. As the Buddha said: "You, yourself, as much as anybody deserve your love and affection."

Do an inventory of your good actions: cases in which you have done well, or tried to do so. Suppose for example that Joe again goes to dinner with Fred and the parents. On that occasion, he deliberately refrains from turning the conversation to his own excellence and successes. He resists the temptation to self-aggrandize. On the contrary, he very subtly draws everyone's attention to some good quality of Fred's. That in itself is a fine achievement worthy of inventory: being thoughtful and sensitive to the needs of others, putting their well-being ahead of his own, doing something positive for them just for their benefit. Doing good for yourself counts as well. If you have faced your fear and made that appointment with the dentist, then make sure to pat yourself on the back.

"The thought manifests as the word. The word manifests as the deed. The deed develops into habit and the habit hardens into character. So watch the thought and its ways with care and let it spring from love, born out of concern for all beings."
– Buddha

Step five: *admission*

"Confession of errors is like a broom which sweeps away the dirt and leaves the surface brighter and clearer. I feel stronger for confession."
– Mahatma Gandhi

On this step, you share your inventory with someone with whom you are prepared to share your most horrifying secrets. If you are in a fellowship, this will most conveniently be your sponsor. If not, then choose someone who is likely to listen attentively, not judge and make helpful observations, perhaps noting things you have may have missed and pointing out connections or patterns that you may not have noticed, perhaps identifying with some of what you say and sharing similar aspects of themselves. It is better not to choose someone who is close to you, such as a family member or best friend, nor someone who could be hurt or upset by your thoughts or feelings about them. Always make sure to explain what you are doing before you share with them, and ask their permission. Choose someone who will not try to analyse you or do therapy on you or put pressure on you to think or do anything.

Openly admitting your defects to another person brings huge relief. It often takes the sting out of them, and it is psychologically very beneficial indeed. It is good for you. It will cement your own acceptance of yourself, warts and all, in your own mind; it will help you feel accepted by and part of humanity. It will also force you to be clear in your own mind about the detailed nature of your defects, to be humble, and to accept that they are very real. Publius Syrus says: "To confess a fault freely is the next thing to being innocent of it". Oscar Wilde tells us: "It is the confession, not the priest, that gives us absolution."

If your higher power is a god, or something you can meaningfully communicate with or talk to, then share your inventory also with her, him or it.

Step five is the beginning of a practice of keeping connected with others around you and not being ashamed of yourself. The fact is that your defects are not of much interest to others, unless you hurt them. They have more important things with which to concern themselves and you will feel better for being aware of this. If you get into the habit of confessing wrongdoings, then you will find yourself indulging in far fewer, your life will be easier and your mind more serene.

"The worst of my actions or conditions seem not so ugly unto me as I find it both ugly and base not to dare to avouch for them."
– Michel Eyquem De Montaigne

Step six: *readiness*

"Large streams from little fountains flow, tall oaks from little acorns grow."
– D. Everett

As said above, overactive, misdirected, unmanaged instincts lead to all kinds of distress directly and indirectly through interactions with others and the world. But most of us are used to the idea that the pursuit of money and what it can buy, of good food, power and the admiration of others are normal goals. Surely anger is natural, and has its value too? Is it really a good idea to try to work on letting all our so-called 'defects' go?

Yes it is.

In reality, anger is a very primitive instinct, evolved for living in the jungle. Acting on it in civilised society leads to no good. As Buddha says: "In a controversy the instant we feel anger we have already ceased striving for the truth, and have begun striving for ourselves." Of course, if you are actually, genuinely under immediate physical threat and need to fight, then a natural surge of anger may provide some needed energy. But when you are not in that situation, it is best to work on living without it, as far as possible. Deal with injustice by the use of careful thought regarding the best course of action, not by stomping and shouting or hitting people.

"Human life is founded on kindness and concord, and is bound into an alliance for common help, not by terror, but by mutual love."
– Seneca

There is nothing wrong with enjoying fine food, sex and the respect and admiration of others, in moderation. But to be positive rather than negative influences, these must come to one in the course of a well-conducted life, as aspects of physically and psychologically healthy pursuits. After all, food is just food and sex just sex. They are necessary for survival and procreation and enjoyable in their own right. But we are very prone to be overly concerned with pursuing them, giving them far more importance than they really have. This leads to dissatisfaction (wanting yet more), time and energy poorly spent, overindulgence, an unhealthy body or unhealthy relationships.

If you are in a justified position of power and influence, through work or otherwise, then you can do good for others by exercising it wisely, and gain satisfaction from so doing. If you seek power for its own sake, then your efforts to use it will not be well-directed, and you will only cause distress to yourself and others. Nobody likes a bully. Don't push people around. Power brings commensurate responsibility. Make sure that it is really what you want, and carefully and honestly examine your motives for wanting it before you seek it.

Money is, of course, necessary for most of us, and can really come in very handy. But do you really need that new dress or bicycle or car, that better room or house, that upgrade of something or other? Would you not be far, far better off being satisfied with what you have and helping someone who is worse off than yourself, maybe starving to death or about to drink themselves into hospital?

If you feel restless, irritable and/or discontent, instead of getting angry, or self-punitive, or despairing, instead of doing something destructive, or nothing at all, do something positive. Take action to make the world a better place. Help yourself by taking inventory and sharing with another, to find out what is really bugging you. Then help someone else.

As you work on the steps, you will become less enslaved or distracted by your primitive, instinctive urges and their manifestations as desires for food and sex, money and power, recognition and praise. You will cease to fear not having enough of these things, and become able fully to enjoy being in the moment you are in. You will become better adapted to living well in the world around you and the plants, animals and people in it. You will grow as a human being and become more serene and joyful as a result.

A giant oak tree does not grow before our eyes. Character development takes time. But it pays huge dividends in the long run. To attain, maintain and increase serenity, you must be entirely ready to let all you defects go, and always to keep working towards that ideal.

"A man does not have to be an angel in order to be saint."
– Albert Schweitzer

Step seven: *humility*

"Humility is truth"
– Desiderius Erasmus

If you live in a street in which everyone has a TV set, and you do not, you are likely to feel deprived. This will cause you distress. Yet, before the 1950s all of humanity got by just fine without any TVs at all. Probably in such a situation it would not be the TV itself that matters so much. It is just not having what others have that is so distressing. True humility would allow you to accept the situation as your lot, be content with what you have and make the most of it. Life can be as rich, or indeed much richer without a TV than with one. After all, there are much better things to do than watch TV. Humility allows you to make the best of what you have, and not suffer from the felt deprivation of not having more.

However much you know, there is much, much more that you could learn. You will learn more if you listen to others than if you tell them what you think they should know. Intellectual humility is a prerequisite of acquiring knowledge and knowledge gives strength.

Emotional security and self-respect cannot be found in the words, deeds and perceptions of others. To feel estimable, it is best to do estimable things, whether others recognize this and praise you for them or not.

There is nothing wrong with taking pride in a job well done. You deserve the praise of others and of yourself when you have done well. It is healthy for you to take pleasure in such praise when it is actually deserved.

But simply being proud of yourself for no reason does you no good at all and is positively unhealthy. How you compare to others and what others think of you really do not matter. However great you are, you could always be better and do better.

It is important to understand also that humility goes with honesty and respect for the truth. So it does not mean that you should represent yourself as lacking good qualities that you in fact possess, as being less than you really are. It does not require you to compare yourself to others one way or another, and certainly not to represent yourself as less than others. Under-confidence is neither healthy nor virtuous. Humility only requires that you recognize that you are just one among others. You are not more important. But nor are you less important. Being humble means showing respect for the truth, and therefore it means being realistic. A good sense of reality will relieve you of the stresses of maintaining an image, whether the image represents you as more than you are, or as less, or as more in some ways and less in others.

As Al Franken said: "It's easier to put on slippers than to carpet the whole world." It is not up to you to fix everything all the time. But being humble means that sometimes you have to swap the slippers for work shoes. Being one among others means that you should recognize and accept that you have a contribution to make to the groups you are in and to the world you inhabit. One should not play the humility card as an excuse for not taking on responsibilities and carrying them out. Overplaying the humility card shows lack of humility, since it allows you to shirk, put up your feet and relax, and leave work to others when you could do it yourself, thus placing your own comfort ahead of the comfort of others.

Humility shows you your place in the universe and is a prerequisite of connectedness with the world around you. Humility is the root of spirituality. Humility brings serenity.

"Do you wish to rise? Begin by descending. You plan a tower that will pierce the clouds? Lay first the foundation of humility."
– Saint Augustine

Step eight: *harms*

"It is very easy to forgive others their mistakes; it takes more grit to forgive them for having witnessed your own."
– Jessamyn West

Step eight consists in making a list of all those we have harmed, and becoming willing to make amends to them all.

Overactive, misdirected instinctive drives cause us to lie, steal, cheat, lash out physically or verbally, make others feel small, or guilty, jealous or neglected. If you have harmed anyone and not yet made it right, you will feel guilty, consciously or unconsciously. To be at peace with yourself you must put things right. This is also another exercise in humility, a practice of being realistic about yourself and becoming willing to live by adjusting yourself to fit the world. Serenity requires it and so does justice. You must practice doing what is right because it is right, in order to fit harmoniously in the world you are so very fortunate to inhabit.

Again it is necessary to be thorough and fearless. The best policy here is: if in doubt, include them. It will do no harm if you attempt to make amends to a person who does not feel that you have harmed them. So you should include those who do or may not know that you think you may have harmed them. But take it easy and don't create any burden for them by insisting that you have done wrong if they think you have not, or being a nuisance in any other way.

Among the most difficult amends to make are to those who, you believe, have harmed you more than you have harmed them. You will really have to swallow your pride and focus just on doing your best to fix any damage that you, yourself, may have caused. Let the other person think what they will about their own actions, or the truth (moral or otherwise) as they see it. You don't have any duty to fix their conscience or help them make right their wrongs, so make sure you do not attempt to do so. It will not further your serenity. Let them deal with those matters. They are not your concern and you need not let them bother you. Rise above it. Do your best to mend the damage you have done and you will gain great self-respect and strength from it.

"To see the right and not to do it is cowardice."
– Confucius

Step nine: *amends*

"One of the most important things to realize is that you only have one life to live. It can all be gone in instant. Cherish each moment and say what you need to say to someone before it's too late."
– Nicole Fickes

On step nine, we make direct amends to all those we have harmed, wherever this is possible, except when to do so would harm them or others.

For many, this step raises difficult moral and practical questions. Good and careful judgement is called for. So it is an excellent idea to seek advice from your sponsor or unofficial advisory board or some other wise counsellor.

Having become willing to make amends to all you have harmed, it is time to take action. There may be those you just cannot contact. Or there may be other reasons why making amends to them is literally impossible. Accept this with serenity.

It is up to you how to make the amends. An apology and complete disclosure (where this will not harm anyone) may suffice. If you have stolen or vandalized or otherwise deprived someone of their property, then you should make full financial amends, or at least offer to do so.

Among those to whom amends are possible, it is best to start with those where it will not be too problematic. Work your way through the list as quickly and efficiently as possible. Be careful not to do any harm: if knowing the truth, or all of it, may hurt someone, then it may be best to refrain from that, and make do with doing something else for them.

When you have completed this step, you should be feeling happy. You should be free of regrets and at peace with yourself and the world. You should feel worth your place in society and on the planet. You should be free of pointless fear. Hence you should be free of any problematic desire for drink or drugs. You should have developed something of a habit of right thinking and right action and not chasing your own ends. Serenity should have found you.

If it hasn't, then have another go at steps four and five. There is almost certainly something still lurking in your mind that needs to be brought to the surface and released.

Carry on to step ten, as well.

"Admitting your mistakes is not a sign of weakness. It shows you have the courage to know you are wrong, and that you have become stronger."
– Aaron DeCamp

Step ten: *perseverance*

"The spiritual life is not a theory. We have to live it."
– Bill Wilson

Steps ten, eleven and twelve are about maintaining psychological well-being and growing spiritually. Step ten is really steps four–nine applied in the now. You will train yourself to spot each emotional disturbance as it arises and to nip incipient problems in the bud. You must immediately put right any wrongs that you do. Be brave. If you catch yourself lying, or hurting someone out of anger or envy or fear, swallow your pride, admit your mistake and apologize straight away. Train yourself to act like a really good human being!

It is a good idea to carry on with a written inventory daily, at least for a while. Look for disturbances to your serenity and try to identify which defect is causing the problem. How have you been self-willed or self-seeking or self-absorbed? Have you, for example, been slothful, greedy or arrogant? Have you been trying to change someone to fit your picture of how things should be? Be objective. This is just fact-finding and psychological engineering. You are a work in progress. Approach the task seriously and take pride in your work. Think about what you could have done better and do not forget the credit side of the inventory: when you have done well, promptly admit it to yourself (try not to admit it to others too much), and make the world a better place by taking due satisfaction from it. Check in and share with your sponsor or equivalent from time to time (as in step five).

It is important to get into the habit of doing inventory online, as you find yourself subject to flare-ups of defects. Do not let your instincts control you. For example, if you get angry, restrain yourself. Do not act on the anger. Breathe deeply and slowly. Calm yourself. Chill. Act calmly and gently. As soon as possible, take a step back from the situation and do a quick inventory on paper or just in your head. Make sure to look out for subtler forms of defective behaviour such as self-aggrandizing, trying to appear better than others, manipulating, sulking, 'constructively' criticising and the like. Make sure to be scrupulously honest with yourself. Check carefully that you have not hidden any bad motives under good ones.

Keep the well-being of others firmly in mind when you act and when you react. If they are being difficult, remember that this may be due to their own suffering, stupidity or ignorance or simply a different understanding of things from your own. Do not let their issues cause you problems. Don't get tangled up in them. Keep your emotional distance and be kind and forgiving. If you do something wrong, admit to it and make it right, straight way.

"Courtesy, kindness, justice and love are the keynotes by which we may come into harmony with practically anybody."
– Bill Wilson

It is much easier to act well if you do all that and if you act well, you will feel well. You will avoid causing yourself unnecessary stress in a quite vain attempt to satisfy a misdirected instinct. Your interactions with others will be easy. You can promote harmony rather than conflict, go with the flow, make others and yourself happy and enjoy the ride.

As time goes by, you may learn to handle your emotions properly all the time, and so have no need to write much down. But it is a good idea every six or twelve months to do an extensive inventory review with your sponsor or someone equivalent, so that you can learn about yourself and see what you could usefully work on more. If at any point you begin to feel irritable, restless and discontent, inventory and a consultation with your sponsor or equivalent are immediately required. Do not let this slip or the price you will likely have to pay could be far more than you can afford.

Stay humble, and, where you find recurring defects, work on improving your performance over time (as in steps seven and six).

"The secret of your future is hidden in your daily routine."
– Mike Murdock

Step eleven: *meditation*

"Meditation can help us embrace our worries, our fear, our anger; and that is very healing. We let our own natural capacity of healing do the work."
– Thich Nhat Hanh

On step eleven you develop your conscious contact with your higher power, and you allow your contact with it to guide you to right action. This should be part of your daily routine.

There are many ways to do this, depending on what your higher power is and what kind of a person you are. If you are religious, then prayer and the study of religious texts will be good. Read the chapter on step eleven in The Twelve Steps and Twelve Traditions of Alcoholics Anonymous (available free online at aa.org).

It is an excellent idea each evening to spend some time reflecting on your spiritual development. If you don't do a written inventory as a matter of routine, consider whether one is needed. Check for any resentment, jealousy, dishonesty, and greed. Is there something you have been putting off that you should have done? Have you neglected any duty to a person or group? In what ways, if any, could you have been less selfish, more kind or beneficial to others? Have you done something for another, expecting nothing for yourself, not even recognition? Have you been good to yourself? What do you need to work on? How can you improve?

Everyone would benefit greatly from adopting a daily practice of mindful meditation. This is now a very common practice among addicts in recovery, whether they are involved in an Anonymous fellowship or not. Get a book, download some videos. Anything by Thich Nhat Hanh is excellent. Join a group. On the Internet, there are many good free guided meditation videos. Take advantage of these.

If you have no experience of meditation and can't immediately find guidance, here is a simple one you can do now. It is an exercise in awareness and acceptance. Don't try hard. Don't worry at all about getting it right or wrong. This is a basic breath meditation.

With bare feet, sit comfortably on a chair, your back straight, head tilted slightly forward. Plant your feet firmly on the floor and feel it for a few moments, to ground yourself. Close your eyes. Relax. Take a few moments, or more, just being. Without making much effort, just turn your attention to being aware of everything that comes within your subjectivity: sounds, thoughts, sensations, whatever appears to you. When you are ready, take three deep, slow breaths. Then just breathe normally. Now focus your attention on your breath. Don't try to breathe any particular way, just continue to breathe. Breathe in and out, inhale and exhale. Notice how the breath flows in and how it flows out. Try to attend only on your breath, on how it feels to you. Your mind will wander. Thoughts of the past may appear, or thoughts of what might yet come to be, or just of make-believe. You may note these as they pass: "there is a thought". Let it go, let it drift off, unfinished. Accept everything that comes to your consciousness. Make no evaluation or judgement. Keep turning your attention back to your breath. Attend to its details. Thoughts will come. Just let them go. Let them fade into the background. Attend to your breath. Attend to its details. Accept, and allow yourself to enjoy the moment. Do enjoy it, as much as you can! Keep on for as long as you wish or feel comfortable.

Even two or three minutes of meditation can be beneficial. The more you practice, the longer you will be able to meditate comfortably, and the more benefit you will derive. Work up to at least twelve minutes a day. You can do a breath meditation –perhaps without the bare feet – at any time that suits you, if you feel like chilling out and letting your mind settle. You can use the same technique attending to ambient sounds, rather than to your breath. Attend only to the sounds. Try not to label them, or identify their causes. Just be aware of their qualities as sounds, as they appear to your consciousness. Be with them. Let the flow around you and in your mind. Be with the sounds. Accept, enjoy. The sounds of moving water are particularly good for this meditation. If you can find a fountain or stream by which to sit, that would be excellent. If you can't find suitable flowing water, the sounds of a city will do. Alternatively, listen to some recorded meditation sounds or music. Either technique – breath or sound - works well when you are travelling in a bus or train or some such.

In general, get into the habit of attending to what is in the world around you, not what is going on in your head. Observe people and take pleasure in the physical environment, in the wonderful creations of your fellow humans, buildings, bridges, statues in a park and take pleasure in nature, in trees, plants, ponds, clouds, and stars. Relax and be in the world.

Be in the world and the answers will come to you.

"Many people are so poor that the only thing they have is money. Cultivate your spiritual growth."
– Rodolfo Costa

"When you arise in the morning think of what a privilege it is to be alive, to think, to enjoy, to love..."

"Dwell on the beauty of life. Watch the stars, and see yourself running with them."
– Marcus Aurelius

Step Twelve: *carrying the message*

"Service to others is the rent you pay for your room here on earth."
– Muhammad Ali

Step twelve bids us to carry the message that as the result of these steps, we have had a spiritual awakening, and to practice the principles of the steps in all our affairs.

Practicing the principles involves the daily practice of steps ten and eleven and don't forget steps six and seven. If you are an addict, do not slack off on these, ever. Sensitization of the dopamine system is permanent. Accept this fact with humility and serenity. This means that having a drink or drug brings ruin and if you don't keep spiritually fit, then you will lose your serenity, your instincts will take over, your dopamine system will kick off, your instincts will run riot and overcome your better judgement, the obsession will return and you will drink or use drugs. Spiritual regress can set in very quickly if you do not keep up your fitness regime. Relapse is often swift and totally devastating.

Carrying the message is part and parcel of you new life. Selflessly helping others is now something you do and by so doing, you carry the message, if only by setting a good example.

Don't impose, push or bully. Do not offer advice where it is not sought. You are not a messiah. You are just another human being. Be humble and unselfish. You are helping others for their sake and not yours, though you do benefit as a result. Never forget that and then you will be able to help them most effectively. You will be better adapted to the social world around you and know serenity as a result.

If you are in an Anonymous fellowship, do service. Helping your group save lives does wonders for one's self-esteem. If you are not in a fellowship, then find a charity or cause you like and work for it. Don't be slothful. There is plenty of work for all of us.

"The best way to find yourself is to lose yourself in the service of others."
– Mahatma Gandhi

Endpiece

Serenity spring

Courage to be our curry

Wisdom our winter

"If you are depressed you are living in the past. If you are fearful and anxious you are living in the future. If you are at peace, you are living in the present moment."
– Lao Tzu

"Be Here Now"
– Ram Dass

"We are not going to change the whole world, but we can change ourselves and feel free as birds. We can be serene even in the midst of calamities and, by our serenity, make others more tranquil. Serenity is contagious. If we smile at someone, he or she will smile back and a smile costs nothing. We should plague everyone with joy. If we are to die in a minute, why not die happily, laughing?"
– Swami Satchidananda